ELEGIE

(In memory of Denis Brain)

for Horn and Piano

by

FRANCIS POULENC

Duration 8 minutes

An E♭ Horn part is available to special order from the publisher.

CHESTER MUSIC

part of **WiseMusic**Group

EXCLUSIVELY DISTRIBUTED BY

1

E L E G I E

FRANCIS POULENC (1957)

for Horn and Piano

2

4

ELEGIE

FRANCIS POULENC (1957)

for Horn and Piano

J. W. C. 1607

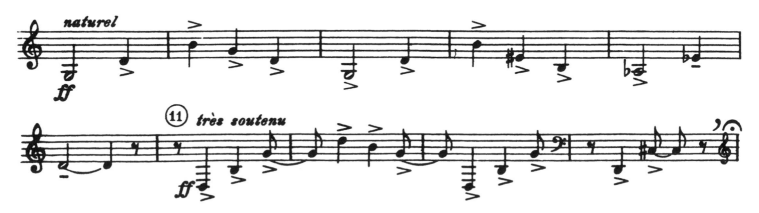

*) respecter le doigté